For with You is the fountain of life; in Your light we see light.

Psalm 36:9

PICTURE BOOK OF
PSALMS

I will give thanks
to You, LORD,
with all my heart;
I will tell of all
Your wonderful
deeds.

Psalm 9:1

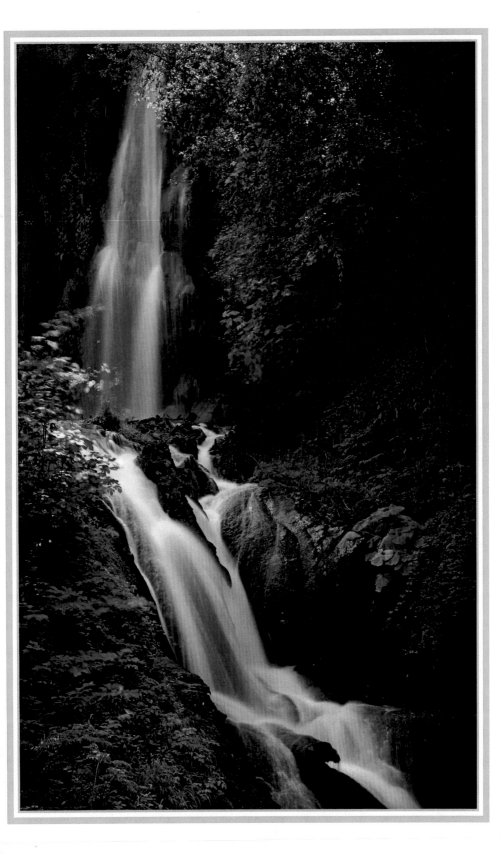

For great is Your love, reaching to the heavens; Your faithfulness reaches to the skies.

Psalm 57:10

The LORD is my shepherd; I shall not want. He makes me lie down in green pastures. He leads me beside still waters. He restores my soul.

Psalm 23:1-3

The LORD is my light and my salvation— whom shall I fear? The Lord is the stronghold of my life— of whom shall I be afraid?

Psalm 27:1

The LORD is my rock, my fortress and my savior; my God is my rock, in whom I find protection. He is my shield, the power that saves me, and my place of safety.

Psalms 18:2

Those who look to
Him are radiant, and
their faces shall
never be ashamed.

Psalm 34:5

He will cover you with his feathers. He will shelter you with his wings. His faithful promises are your armor and protection.

Psalm 91:4

Delight yourself in the LORD, and He will give you the desires of your heart.

Psalm 37:4

God is our refuge and strength, an ever-present help in trouble.

Psalm 46:1

Your word is a lamp for my feet, a light on my path.

Psalm 119:105

Be still and know that I am God.

Psalm 46:10

Cast your cares on the LORD and he will sustain you.

Psalm 55:22

I keep my eyes always on the LORD. With him at my right hand, I will not be shaken.

Psalm 16:8

The heavens declare the glory of God; the skies proclaim the work of his hands.

Psalm 19:1

This is the day that
the LORD has made;
let us rejoice and be
glad in it.

Psalm 118:24

In peace I will lie down and sleep, for You alone, LORD, make me dwell in safety.

Psalm 4:8

You make known to me the path of life; You will fill me with joy in Your presence, with eternal pleasures at Your right hand.

Psalm 16:11

LORD my God, I called to You for help, and You healed me.

Psalm 30:2

But I trust in Your unfailing love; my heart rejoices in Your salvation.

Psalm 13:5

Made in United States
North Haven, CT
16 May 2024

52587644R00024